LOVE HIJACKED

Return to
Your First Love
Before It's Too Late

KADE YOUNG

Copyright © 2025 by Kade Young

All rights reserved. No part of this book may be reproduced in any form by an electronic or mechanical means, including information storage and retrieval systems, without permission in writing from the copyright owner, except by a reviewer who may quote brief passages in a review.

Questions or bulk orders? Contact books@kadeyoung.com

ISBN (Paperback): 978-1-7377322-8-0

Scripture quotations marked NLT are taken from the Holy Bible, New Living Translation, copyright © 1996, 2004, 2015 by Tyndale House Foundation. Used by permission of Tyndale House Publishers, Inc., Carol Stream, Illinois 60188. All rights reserved. Scripture quotations marked NKJV are taken from the New King James Version®. Copyright © 1982 by Thomas Nelson. Used by permission. All rights reserved. Scripture quotations marked AMPC are taken from the Amplified Bible, Copyright © 1954, 1958, 1962, 1964, 1965, 1987 by The Lockman Foundation. Used by Permission.

Contents

1. Exposing Counterfeit Love   1
2. Love Is Kind While Patiently Waiting   3
3. Love Is Not Jealous   5
4. Love Is Not Self-Focused   7
5. Love Is Not Irritable   9
6. Love Only Thinks on Good Things   11
7. Love Doesn't Celebrate Sin   15
8. Love Refuses to Gossip   17
9. Love Gifts Trust   19
10. Love Replaces Criticism with Hope   23
11. Love Doesn't Bail   25
12. Fight for Love   27

1
Exposing Counterfeit Love

L ove. What a loaded word.

We throw it around haphazardly without understanding its power. We act so confident in our understanding of love, yet we know so little about it.

We are so bombarded with Satan's counterfeit love that it has become a stronghold. We struggle to escape the perversion that is infecting every relationship we have.

This book marks the end of the struggle. Allow God's Word to come in like a sword and cut off every bit of counterfeit love.

Love Comes First

The Bible reveals that love is more important than prophecy and the gifts of the spirit. Actually, without love, all the gifts of the Spirit are meaningless.

The Bible also reveals that love is more important than knowledge. In other words, what you know about the Bible is meaningless without love.

In God's eyes, love is even greater than faith. It's not that faith isn't important; it is just pointless without love.

If you want to serve God well, love comes first.

It's so important that you might as well set everything else aside and focus on love until you get it.

We know this because 1 Corinthians 13 is one of our go tos in the church. The problem is we know it, but we don't do it. And the evidence is in our actions.

The things listed about love in 1 Corinthians 13 are not unattainable. It wasn't written to show that we would never measure up.

It was written for clarity so we can demonstrate God's love for the world.

If you've been in church for long, you've heard these things many times before. But don't daze off just because it's familiar. Instead, read with focus and be corrected on the things you know but are not doing.

Break Every Stronghold

As you read these short chapters, you'll have an opportunity at the end of each one to repent and break the stronghold that is keeping you from true love.

If you discover an area where you want freedom, respond quickly. There is a work the Holy Spirit wants to do within you, but it requires your response.

2
Love Is Kind While Patiently Waiting

<u>1 Corinthians 13:4 NKJV</u> – Love suffers long and is kind.

We often separate these two, but they go together. Not only is love long-suffering (patient), but **it is kind while it is patient.**

Do you know what this phrase "long-suffering" really means?

To be patient in bearing the offenses and injuries of others. Here's how it is explained in Ephesians:

> <u>Ephesians 4:2 NLT</u> - Always be humble and gentle. Be patient with each other, making allowance for each other's faults because of your love.

Make room for the faults of others, recognizing that you, too, have faults.

It's not that you ignore them. But when those faults come to the surface, approach resolve with patience, kindness, and gentleness.

If you tend to get upset with others' faults and you are ready to break that stronghold, surrender it to God right now.

If you tend to ignore others' faults instead of finding resolve with patience, kindness, and gentleness, make a commitment right now to embrace the uncomfortable conversation.

3

Love Is Not Jealous

1 Corinthians 13:4 NKJV – Love does not envy.

Here we find ourselves all the way back to number ten of the Ten Commandments: You shall not covet.

Every time you get jealous of what someone else has, not only are you breaking one of the Ten Commandments, but you are abandoning the most important part of your Christian walk: love.

Do you get upset when someone else gets a promotion?

Are you upset with those who make more money than you?

How about that person who got the car that you wanted?

This is a hard thing to admit. But, it's time to break the stronghold.

If you want freedom from covetousness, deny your pride, repent, and ask God to help you celebrate others' successes.

4

Love Is Not Self-Focused

1 Corinthians 13:4-5 NKJV – Love does not parade itself, is not puffed up; does not behave rudely, does not seek its own.

Have you ever been around someone who constantly talks about themselves and what they have accomplished? It's exhausting because it's ungodly behavior.

This is an extreme case. But the reality is, most Christians are bound by self. It is the most flaunted expression of counterfeit love.

In our present culture, everything is about me, myself and I.

Pamper yourself. Put yourself first. Make sure to get your me time. Put your mark on the earth. Don't let anyone else get in your way. You do you!

The best way to figure out if you are infected with this is to ask yourself a question: **Am I more interested in others than I am myself?**

When you meet with someone, are you consumed with what you will say? Or are you more interested in learning what they have to say?

In other words, would you be okay simply sitting there, asking questions about them, and listening?

The solution for this is simple: Get curious about others.

Find out what they are up to. Find out what they are trying to accomplish. Find out how you can help them reach their goals.

If you want the Holy Spirit to start correcting you every time you get consumed with self, opt in now by praying, "Holy Spirit, do what it takes to rid me of selfishness."

5

Love Is Not Irritable

<u>1 Corinthians 13:5 NKJV</u> – Love is not provoked.

Do you know what this is saying? **Love is not irritable.**

If it's easy to make you upset, today everything changes. That's not who you are.

The enemy would love for you to believe this is how you are wired. But that's not true.

Since God placed His love on the inside of you, you are more than capable of doing this.

If you are done being irritable, if you are done being one of those people who just flies off the handle, lift up your hands and surrender it to the Lord.

Pray this out loud, "I am done being irritable. I rebuke the lie that this is my personality. It is not who I am. I am full of peace and patience in Christ."

6
Love Only Thinks on Good Things

1 Corinthians 13:5 NKJV – Love thinks no evil.

What would be considered an evil thought?

You probably go to the extreme of thinking it refers to lust and perversion and hate and violence. But the reality is, **any ungodly thought is an evil thought.**

Early in my marriage, I would sit and think about everything Beth was doing wrong and how our marriage would be so much better if she changed. Interestingly, I couldn't see that I was the problem.

When you rehearse your spouse's faults, or anyone's faults for that matter, it would be considered evil thinking.

Nowhere does God say to consume yourself with others' faults.

Several years ago, I was lying in bed rehearsing what I had done wrong. I made a mistake in one of my work projects, and I was playing it over and over again.

I was thinking, "I can't believe I did that. What is my boss going to think when I tell him? I'm such an idiot. How did I not see that? I deserve to be tormented with guilt."

I had been doing this my whole life! I was consumed with my own failures. But this time, the Holy Spirit interrupted my pity party by reminding me of a scripture I had read many times.

> **Philippians 4:8 NLT** - Fix your thoughts on what is true, and honorable, and right, and pure, and lovely, and admirable. Think about things that are excellent and worthy of praise.

This time, I received revelation from this familiar scripture.

Any thought that does not pass every condition in this test is ungodly. Allowing ungodly thoughts to continue is sin.

Love thinks no evil.

We are not talking about ungodly thoughts that you take captive. We are talking about ungodly thoughts you rehearse when you mull over others' faults or your own.

Aren't you glad God doesn't do that? So, let's line up with Him and only think on things that are excellent and worthy of praise. Here's how we do it:

> **2 Corinthians 10:5 NKJV** - Bring every thought into captivity to the obedience of Christ.

This is an ongoing choice you have to make. When an evil thought comes on the scene, cast it out. Don't allow it to take up residence in your mind. Replace it with godly thoughts.

There's no shortcut for this. Renewing your mind is ongoing work. You have to put in the effort. You have to become the master of your own mind.

It's up to you.

7
Love Doesn't Celebrate Sin

<u>1 Corinthians 13:5-6 NKJV</u> – Love does not rejoice in iniquity, but rejoices in the truth.

This is where the "love is love" argument falls apart. Iniquity, also known as sin, does not mesh with love. Love and iniquity do not go together. If iniquity is involved, it is counterfeit love.

If you have sex outside of marriage, it is counterfeit love. If you have premarital sex, it is counterfeit love. If you engage in LGBTQ behaviors, it is counterfeit love.

When iniquity is involved, you can be sure that God's love is nowhere to be found.

In order to experience God's love, you must live according to the truth found in the Bible.

This requires discipline. You have to crucify your flesh. You have to remove yourself from ungodly behaviors.

Philippians 2:13 NLT – For God is working in you, giving you the desire and the power to do what pleases him.

You are not on your own. God is updating your desires and giving you power to live free from sin. You just need to cooperate.

8
Love Refuses to Gossip

<u>1 Corinthians 13:7 NKJV</u> – Love bears all things.

This one is somewhat mysterious, so let's dig in and ensure we get it. Every detail in scripture is important. In a practical application, the original Greek word translated to "bear" refers to a roof protecting the inside of a home. Here is the definition according to the Thayer Lexicon:

- To protect by covering.

- To cover with silence; to conceal the faults of others.

- To keep off something that threatens.

What does this look like in everyday life?

The Bible instructs us to confess our sins to each other so we can find healing. But it doesn't say to confess the sins of someone else, not even if it is disguised as a prayer request.

The faults of someone else are not yours to talk about.

As a matter of fact, God's kind of love provides a covering of silence while they sort it out.

When you find yourself talking about someone else's faults to anyone other than that person, you are in sin. You are working outside of God's love. You are hindering the body of Christ.

The church should be a place where we can go to someone, confess our sins, find healing, and trust that they will never say a word about it.

Others' sins are not yours to share. Your job is to conceal their faults and protect them with a covering of silence. If they want to share, that's up to them!

The best way you can help them find healing is by creating a protective covering over them while they work it out. We all know that gossip doesn't help someone overcome sin.

Do you need to confess the sin of gossip so you can be healed? If so, call up a fellow believer and do it now.

Love Gifts Trust

1 Corinthians 13:7 NKJV – Love believes all things.

This is another mysterious statement that we tend to brush over. So, let's dig in and make sure we get it this time.

This is the same word used to talk about someone believing in Christ. That makes this even more challenging to wrap your head around because we are talking about believing in people.

There are three definitions of this Greek word that bring clarity:

- To place confidence in

- To trust

- To commit

Have you seen the movie *The Blind Side*? A foster-care child called "Big Mike" had the odds stacked against him. No one seemed to care until an unlikely family took him in.

His new adoptive parents faced the challenges with him, helping him overcome one painful step at a time. It wasn't an easy road, but he eventually made his way to the NFL as an offensive lineman.

We all love stories of the underdogs rising to the top. But we often forget about the key ingredient to their success—the good Samaritan who did what no one else was willing to do.

With no leg to stand on, the good Samaritan gives them the gift of placing their confidence in who they could become. They offer trust without requiring them to earn it. They commit to the process without wavering.

We love this story because it is God's love on display. It touches the deepest part of our innermost being because our spirits recognize, this is real love.

Yet we've adopted a totally different mindset.

We're convinced that people have to earn our trust. We aren't going to place confidence in them until they give us a good reason to!

And commitment? We would rather keep our options open than be tied down by our commitments.

We all have some work to do on this one, and it starts at home.

Give your spouse the gift of your confidence in who they will become. Give them the gift of trust without earning it. Commit to the process no matter how challenging it is.

Do the same for your kids. Do the same for your parents. Do the same for your church family. Do the same for God.

Of everything you've read so far, I imagine this is the most challenging. That's why you must first give God the gift of trust.

Trust what He says in His Word, even when you don't like it. When you don't understand, trust anyway. When it is contrary to the world's wisdom, trust anyway.

Give the gift of trust.

10
Love Replaces Criticism with Hope

<u>1 Corinthians 13:7 NKJV</u> – Love hopes all things.

Now we are tying it all together. This gives us the picture of patiently waiting for someone to become who they were meant to be.

And we're not waiting with our arms crossed, full of criticism. We are waiting with joy, full of confidence that they will make it, and giving them the gift of trust every step of the way.

A person who loves as God loves is someone you can confide in. Someone who cheers you on toward the goal. Someone who helps you along the way.

It's not that they never confront you. They do. They rejoice in the truth! They share truth with kindness and the expectation that you can do it.

They don't put you down, they lift you into the truth.

Love refuses to criticize and instead chooses to remain hopeful.

Love hopes ALL things.

11

Love Doesn't Bail

<u>1 Corinthians 13:7 NKJV</u> – Love endures all things.

It's not a mistake that this is the last thing listed. It is the bow tied around the beautiful love package. It's what holds it all together.

It also echos the very first thing that was written: Love is patient.

Patient endurance is what holds love together.

In order to love as God loves, you must resist the urge to bail. You must persevere through many trials. You must stay calm and confident when it looks like they aren't going to make it.

Love sticks it out, not in a hopeless mess, but in confident hope no matter how long it takes.

Is there anyone you have given up on?

Take some time now to allow God to restore your hope. Fix your thoughts on who God created them to be, not who they are right now.

12

Fight for Love

The most challenging thing we will ever do is love as God loves.

Our flesh hates it. Satan hates it. The world hates it.

Everything ungodly is waging war against true love.

But God has demonstrated His love for you by giving His one and only Son as a sacrifice for your sins.

He is beyond patient with your nonsense. He thinks no evil about you.

God remains confident in your outcome even when you are acting like a fool. He gives you the gift of trust even though you didn't earn it.

He endures your faults as you work through them one step at a time.

God demonstrates His love for you so you can love others the same way He loves you.

Yes, it is a fight to love as God loves. But it is a fight He has equipped you to win.

The things in this book are not unattainable. They weren't written in 1 Corinthians 13 to show that we would never measure up. They were written for clarity so we can demonstrate God's love for the world.

Are you ready to lean into the power of the Holy Spirit as you choose to love like He loves?

You can't do this without the Holy Spirit. You must be full of Him to love as God loves.

If you want a fresh filling of the Holy Spirit, or even if you want to be filled for the first time, ask Him to fill you now.

Pray this, "Holy Spirit, I need your help. Fill me with Your power to love like God loves. I receive it now in the name of Jesus."

Next Step

I'd like to personally invite you to join my email list, where I seek the Lord daily to craft short, powerful messages that ignite great boldness for Jesus.

Sign up for free at kadeyoung.com.

About the Author
KADE YOUNG

K**ade Young** has one mission: to help believers break free from powerless Christianity and step into bold faith. As an apostle of Jesus Christ, he writes quick, hard-hitting reads that ignite boldness, activate miracles, and reveal what it truly means to walk in the Spirit.

He leads NoLimits Church, equipping believers to walk in supernatural authority, and founded Collaborate Worship, helping churches worldwide create incredible sound for powerful worship.

Beyond ministry, Kade is a husband, a father of six, and a newbie farmer on a wild adventure raising sheep, cattle, and chickens with his family.

Learn more at **kadeyoung.com**

More Books by Kade Young

7 Spirits of God

Unlocking the Fullness of the Holy Spirit

Jesus Ain't Woke

Your Wake-Up Call to Stop Tolerating Sin and Embrace the Transforming Power of Jesus Christ

God's End-Time Wealth Transfer

Position Yourself to Receive Great Wealth to Fund the End-Time Harvest

Ancient Roots of the LGBTQ Movement

Exposing the Demonic War on Gender, Sexuality, and Biblical Truth

Order books on Amazon or at kadeyoung.com

www.ingramcontent.com/pod-product-compliance
Lightning Source LLC
Chambersburg PA
CBHW071256070526
44583CB00017B/2495